FEED THE PIG, NOT THE BILL COLLECTORS

FEED THE PIG, NOT THE BILL COLLECTORS:
Guide to Real Debt Solutions and Personal Saving Habits

First Printing, 2015

ISBN-13: 978-1508690573
ISBN-10: 150869057X

The advice provided in this book is general advice only. It has
been prepared without taking into account your objectives,
financial situation or needs. Before acting on this advice you
should consider the appropriateness of the advice, having
regard to your own objectives, financial situation and needs.

TABLE OF CONTENTS

PREFACE

Everyone looks for an opportunity to become financially free. Free from debt, free from harassing phone calls from companies wanting money that you owe them. Freedom of knowing you have an abundance of money stockpiled in a bank vault. The truth is this dream is not farfetched but is not easy to achieve. The harsh reality is if you are in serious debt and do not change then your financial situation won't change. Sitting at the kitchen table staring at your bank account without a plan of action changes nothing. In this book you will be given a plan of action. Your life needs and deserves an overhaul. I want to see your debts paid off and your savings accounts flourish but it starts with you and your attitude.

FEED THE PIG, NOT THE BILL COLLECTORS:

Guide to Real Debt Solutions and Personal Savings Habits

INTRODUCTION TO A NEW YOU

Many books will tell you how to get out of debt fast or become a millionaire overnight. How correct are these sources? Have you ever read these schemes that large companies profiting from book sales call legitimate? The truth is unless you are now a millionaire, becoming a millionaire will not happen overnight. This book will not guarantee a ticket to be a member in the 1% in the economic asset breakdown. It will help you achieve most of your goals and give you financial security. Stop wasting your money one get-rich-quick schemes, pyramid schemes and other things that bring people in with the thought of a luxurious life overnight. Remember if it's too good to be true, it usually isn't true. Authors who write these books with subjects on becoming a millionaire weren't millionaires until they wrote these books. People similar to us made them millionaires.

If you were rich you wouldn't need this book to gain knowledge to instruct you on how to restructure your finances. Assuming you need help be sure you read and keep all the information I'm about to give you because it will help you enjoy money instead of money being the enemy. Everyone has experienced financial troubles and the decisions you make and the knowledge you keep and put into practice will either send your paychecks into someone else's hands or become your paychecks to keep and save for your goals. Don't let a paycheck to paycheck lifestyle hinder your plan to being free from putting money into a collectors pocket.

You need a plan of action and the motivation to enforce the plan to its entirety. To be debt free and be able to enjoy your money is not a handout but something that needs work and dedication also If you want to save for nice things or go on nice vacations, buy a new car, you must focus on restructuring your finances to achieve this freedom.

Pay off your debts and save your paychecks is the only 2 steps throughout this book but are broken into many categories of debt solutions and savings. You need to budget and do it properly, which will make you aware of where your paycheck is going. To create a budget and stick to is one of the hardest tasks you will face until you have gotten use to the fact that overspending is never acceptable. Debt solutions and savings don't have to be painful. To create a balanced budget takes practice and consistency. Things will happen that cause your budget to become unbalanced. You need to want the end prize enough to want to get back on track with your budget making the changes needed to balance your budget once again.

In this introductory chapter I want to point out a crucial product to stay away from, pay day loans. If one item in your budget will tie up a huge sum of your cash, it's pay day loans. These companies are at every corner in town, on the internet and will pull you in with their "No Credit Check" banners on the web. Companies that offer pay day loans capitalize their funds by issuing their consumers a loan that you, by contract, will pay back with interest as high as 1000%. So getting a quick loan for $500 appears good and legit until they send the check you gave them when you received the loan for $700. Pay day loans are a trap and if not controlled will cost you hundreds of dollars per paycheck.

I cannot force you to act on your personal circumstances and I don't know your financial state, so is bankruptcy a good start? This is something I cannot decide for you. With everyone's financial state being different it will be negligent of me to say yes go ahead and file bankruptcy. How to decide is a question that may come to your mind. This book is talking about eliminating debts and saving so after reading these chapters and looking at a well prepared budget it's your responsibility to say "I've got too much debt for my income" or "this is a manageable debt I can pay off in time". This decision is tough but you need to think about the pros and cons and match them with your financial goals. If you do not need credit or you currently own a house and car and need not apply for credit in the next few years then it may be an option but be careful your assets aren't at risk in the bankruptcy. If you're looking to buy a new house or a new car I wouldn't recommend a bankruptcy.

Debt consolidation may be another choice but again you should look at your budget and ask if it's best for you. If you've got good credit but are looking to restructure your finances, debt consolidation may not help your good credit but instead lower it. Everyone's circumstances are different and to get a hold of your finances and balance a budget correctly and work towards becoming debt free, you have to be sick of giving your checks away and making the CEO at a loan company rich. This is difficult, but it will be worth it.

Before we move to the next chapter we need to talk about credit. It is easy for a millionaire to write a book and say no one needs credit and to pay for everything cash. I disagree, credit has been around for centuries because not everyone has the money in porcelain piggy banks to buy a house or a new car. It is unfair for someone wealthy to say that to be happy paying for everything in cash is the only way to be happy. I'll tell you that in secret even these guys need credit. In the chapters that follow, you will learn to use credit to your benefit but use intelligent thinking when using credit. Keep the information and practice the information you keep. Be sure to follow the steps. Each step is a building block and if you leave one step out the entire plan will fail.

THE COST OF A HABIT

In every financial book you read about managing personal finances you always see the first step as expense tracking. Nearly all of them will tell you to keep doing what you are doing and track where your money is going. This is a very important step towards paying off your debts and saving your money but I disagree with the first part of this step. You are here because you want to change so how can I ask you to continue to practice all of your bad habits for a couple more months, risking your finances for 60 more days. Another problem is accuracy. If I tell you to do the same thing you were doing and to watch it, your brain will tell you not to do things you would do because you have the will to change your spending habits. Make sense? My advice is to go to your bank and look at the last 60 days of transactions that occurred before you bought this book. You were most likely on a spending frenzy. Once you have the statements, read them over and categorize on a piece of paper every transaction; fuel, grocery, entertainment, car maintenance or home maintenance, addiction, utilities, insurance, clubs or membership, joy shopping, etc. You can add more categories but this will give you an idea of where your money is going when your lack of financial accountability is causing a financial catastrophe.

It will shock you if your habits were similar to mine, the amount of money you waste in a month and you don't even realize it. How many times did you go to a local gas station and make a purchase for four dollars or go to McDonalds to spend five dollars you thought nothing about while paying for your meal? If you do not use the right discipline to track your expenses and learn to say "no" to some purchases, I can assume you see this happening on your bank statement as you inspect it. Your first step once you list every transaction into categories is to review every transaction and decide whether it was a need, want or maybe you don't know what the transaction is. As you go through your list, you need to decide if you want to continue with the purchases you want in your impulsive spending habits or if you need to cut them from your budget and pay off your debts and save.

Two purchases that people experience a hard time cutting from their budget is tobacco and alcohol. I understand that it's an addiction and I do not specialize in tobacco cessation counseling, so I cannot tell you to quit. There are other options like vapor alternatives. Most people who smoke cigarettes or use smokeless tobacco are afraid to try it because they're unsure of the health risk due to the limited research available. You have to be realistic, every time you inhale a cigarette you are inhaling thousands of chemicals so health should not be your focus but the cost savings. You are reading this book, to save money and improve your life. So let's use cigarettes as an example, if you smoke one pack a day and each pack is on average five dollars a pack, you are inhaling $1,800 per year. The figure is an average for one individual so if there's two smokers in the house, the figure needs to be doubled. That's a vacation, or debts paid. Switching to a vapor alternative by purchasing a basic kit through a vapor retailer may be a higher initial investment for the supplies needed to begin. The average monthly cost for the liquid alternative and maintenance of your device is around $25 a month. That is what you were spending in 5 days. The savings while subtracting the initial buy of a kit is roughly $1,500 a year. You need to explore your options to cut down on this cost for any addiction. Whether it's changing your smoking habits or switching to an alternative or cutting back on the alcohol consumption. This is a huge burden on your budget and cutting it out of your budget will maximize your ability to pay off your debts and save your money.

Impulsive spending is a symptom of poor money management. Learn to use intelligent thinking instead of impulsive thinking whenever you will make any purchase. If you go to a store every week and find a shirt or a new video game, something that entices you and you spend an example sum of $35 a week on your shopping spree then calculate your yearly loss for this habit you find that $1,800 is taken from your potential savings. This is as destructive to your finances as smoking a pack of cigarettes a day. If you are an impulsive shopper I want you to walk around your house and search through your cupboards and walk through your closets and see what items you bought that are still in its original packing or hanging up with the store tag still intact. If there's several items still in the package or with tags still on them or maybe they're items you purchased but used once or twice, how does this make you feel? I want you to remember, if you can, how much these items cost when you purchased them. Could this money have been more useful somewhere else in your budget instead of put away and forgotten? Once you finish this book and a budget set, withdraw the cash you allow yourself for joy shopping and put it in an envelope or wallet separate from where you keep your debit or credit cards. When you go shopping, take the wallet with the allotted sum of cash in it and leave your debit and credit cards at home. Think before your purchase, do I need this? Is this something I'll use and when? Be smart with your money because once you make a purchase you cannot resale an item from a store for the same price you paid for it.

You can similarly find other areas that need to be reduced or cut out of your spending habits such as fast food, soda beverages, entertainment and club memberships. If you got a problem with eating at McDonalds three times a week, you will see cutting this from your budget will free up large amounts of money. One person eating any fast food two times a week spends $500 year. That may not look like a lot but that is $500 you are giving someone for food you don't need. If you're a weekend warrior and enjoy going out for the weekend you need to set your allotted amount for each week and take that amount, leaving your debit and credit cards at home. You'll spend $1000 a year spending $20 a week on your entertainment.

Focus your attention on cutting back on unnecessary spending. If this means locking up your debit card in a storage cabinet or giving it to a trusted family member to hold on to then it's necessary to take every step to control your spending habits. Think about what's in your cart before you make the buy. If it's not a need, it's a want, so you need to decide if your wants now will hinder your goals set for financial stability later. This plan of action as you will see later does not cut out this spending but will control it. If you don't have money to put into your savings after every bill is paid, too many and unnecessary purchases are not a choice right now. Be accountable for your everyday spending and stick to your budget plan.

THE BANK ROBBER: E-COMMERCE

Manufacturers and retailers around the world use a convenient tool to capitalize their revenue, the internet. Until you learn from past mistakes in creating and maintaining and balancing a budget that includes an increasing savings plan, stay away from e-commerce. It is so easy now to get on the internet and search the internet for products you do not need but you want and with free shipping and discounted rates you purchase the item. If you need an item and want to search the internet for a sale, take 24 hours and think if you need the item or if it's a "want" you think you need now. If you review your financial circumstances and mull over the purchase for 24 hours most of the time you discover you do not need the item.

You are here to save yourself from a financial catastrophe. You need to explore every option to save money. This may include using coupons at a local grocery store and buying generic or store brand items. If you receive an advertiser or newspaper, remove the coupon section. While looking through the coupons find items you need. Keep these coupons in a wallet or notebook when you go to the grocery store. Every time you go to the grocery store you need to make a list of what you need throughout the week. Once you make a list, be sure to stick to the list without cheating. Buy nothing that isn't on the list. To begin this habit will cause you to exceed your allotted total for groceries per month. If children are normally with you during your shopping trips, I encourage you to leave them with your spouse or a relative while grocery shopping. Children want items that entice them with company marketing techniques, items similar to cereal and snacks. Instead go alone with your list and find the items you need on the list with no other influence. If you forgot to add something to the list, please write it on a piece of paper and get it next time. This will teach you discipline while grocery shopping. If it's an absolute necessity such as formula for an infant or a medication item go ahead and buy it but write it on a piece of paper so you will remember to add to it next week. When you find an item on your list on the shelf, find the generic or store brand. These items are on average 25-30% cheaper. If you brought a coupon for a name brand item have a calculator handy and do the math. Which is cheaper, the name brand with the coupon or the generic? This is the mentality you should have while grocery shopping and this will become a habit over time saving you hundreds of dollars.

Something that worries most people when looking at their finances is gas prices. This is important but the budget category for a vehicle goes slightly farther than the fuel to run the engine. Remember your routine maintenance needs such as oil changes every few thousand miles, windshield wipers and fluids to name a few. People don't like to budget for these services because they occur every few months. The truth is when they need these things they fail to complete these tasks because they don't include this money into their budget. Your vehicle should be a priority on your budget for maintenance. If you don't get routine oil changes your gas mileage declines causing your budget for gasoline to increase. You risk car issues that are preventable and can take thousands of dollars from your savings to repair. In the long run it's worth it to stay on top of your obligation to service your vehicle to save preventable cost later.

I want you to begin fresh with your debt. You need to get your credit accounts together in front of you in paper form and line them up in ascending order. The credit account with the lowest balance gets paid off first while making the minimum payments on all the other credit accounts. Once that account is paid off keep the card because I am not rich so I understand you need credit for large purchases so you will use this credit card but not for entertainment and shopping sprees. I will explain this later in the book. You have one card paid off so let's focus on the others. The next lowest credit account whether a loan or credit card is the next to be paid. You will pay off your accounts in ascending order using the amount you listed in your budget and any extra funds you come across keeping the credit cards placed in a secure location for now. Paying off your credit accounts will give you a fresh start in managing your credit and I will talk about what to use your credit cards for later in the book.

To finish up this chapter I want to talk about an overlooked problem people face when they see progress in their financial management. If you have access to the computer or the internet, which is probable if you purchased this book, I need you to use a search engine to find a reputable source to view your credit report. Once you pulled up your credit report I want you to find any debt that is delinquent. These accounts may be credit cards you didn't pay or a loan on a repossessed car but can cause traumatic consequences later on if they are disregarded. I want your experience in financial management to be productive and successful so take the time to list the creditor, the total you owe them and find a phone number for the creditor. It is essential to place funds in a savings account to pay these accounts off. Creditors will close an account and two years later after the credit account is forgotten file a civil lawsuit in your county court to place a claim on the delinquent balance plus attorney fees and court cost. The resolution to the complaint is virtually always a garnishment to your paycheck of up to% 25. You cannot afford this and will take away the motivation you've gained to improve your financial wellness. Contact these creditors and question a settlement amount. Most likely the account is with a collection agency and the person you talk to will tell you anything to collect the money before the end of the month. Debt collectors work for a commission, and will pressure you into paying the full amount by the end of the month even if it's a couple days away. It's an unfair practice but stick to your budget because they will most of the time take the same settlement if it's available to begin their next months commission. Once they offer a settlement and you agree to the amount and date, ask for it in writing, whether by email, fax or mail. Avoid legal action against you so you can put these delinquent debts behind you.

HIDDEN DINERO

To save money you didn't know was available will impact your finances considerably over time. Utilities are a good start when looking to save money. Go around your house into every room that comprise a plumbing fixture such as a sink, tub, shower or toilet and listen. If you hear any running water then you need to fix the issue causing the water flow whether it's water dripping or a steady flow of water because the numbers on your water meter are turning. Limit your baths or your bath water levels. Using the shower or bathing consumes water and electric or natural gas to heat the water used. Limit the time you shower which may be impossible if you have teenagers in the house but it's necessary. To save five dollars a month on your bill is $60 a year to put in your savings. The $60 doesn't appear to be a lot but you will save more if you take proper steps to save your water and sewage usage. During the summer months use natural rain water to water your garden and grass instead of your hose. The first year buy a rain barrel to place at the end of your gutter structure. This may be pricey at first but the overall cost will be a bill decrease during the summer months in the following year. Use common sense when using water consumption. If water is running then your meter is turning.

If it's dark outside take a walk around your house. How many lights are on in your house and no one occupying the room? This is common but the electric company is profiting from this negligence. Turn off lights in rooms that are empty and unplug any fixture or charging device that's not being used. If it's plugged in assume it will use electricity in low amounts. Set your thermostat for your air conditioner and furnace to a constant temperature. This is important because changing the setting for the thermostat regularly is overworking your furnace and air conditioning unit which causes your electric bill to sky rocket. This also overworks your temperature control units, replacing this unit is not an expense that is necessary while you are working to put more money in your pockets. If your appliances are old, put an alotted amount into a savings account with your budget plan to replace them with energy efficient appliances. To make a large purchase similar to this looks like you are achieving the opposite of saving money but the reason is the ability to save in the long run. If you pay off your debts and still use appliances that are causing an excessive burden on your electric or water bill you aren't able to save every penny that is available. These purchases will pay for themselves.

Think about the average family's budget and you will see most use a mobile carrier they pay for their cell phone service. If you walk into the living room of many households you will see the television on with service provided by a service provider. We also assume everyone who owns a car is paying auto insurance. These bills can be expensive and the people who pay them are used to sending this money in every month. With the average household relying on these services, they see them as necessities and maybe they are to you. You need knowledge for these services and products to get the most for the least cost. Get your mobile phone bill out and search for things such as "data". If you are paying for 10 gigabytes of data but are using 3 gigabytes you are paying $15 extra a month for something you don't even use. The same thing happens with Cable or satellite if your service includes the movie stations and watch them once a month you are paying for added services you don't use. Contact your mobile service provider and your cable or satellite provider and explain that your bill is too high and that you need to see every available option to decrease the amount of your bill. They want your money and will do whatever to help you so you won't switch to another provider. If they will not help you in decreasing your bill I say that you search other providers and see what they offer. You can save hundreds of dollars a year by either negotiating your payment or switching to a provider with a more affordable choice. Insurance companies will not budge on their annual cost so it does not hurt to complete free online quotes with other companies to find another insurance policy with the same options for a cheaper price.

If you own a home I suggest refinancing if you are qualified. If you can shorten the term of your mortgage you can save thousands of dollars depending on the time left on the loan by increasing your payment . What I will not recommend is requesting more than what is owed on your mortgage.

People who refinance for an amount above what they owe on their mortgage are tempted to spend the money on purchases that are unnecessary and can be bought with cash if they would create an affective budget. This same example can be used for auto loans or student loans. You want to get out of debt the most efficient and comfortable way possible. That means if your mortgage payment is $800 don't agree to pay $1200 a month if you were struggling with the lesser payment. Know what you can pay as a maximum amount with ease before you decide on the refinancing option.

To help you in gaining more funds to increase your success at paying off your debts it wouldn't be a bad idea to take a walk around the house looking for items that could be sold. People get so used to seeing an item they bought but never use they stop paying attention to the item. If you search around your house or garage looking for items you don't use anymore my guess is you will find hundreds of items. Items you pass by everyday but don't pay attention to anymore should be sold because they are not being used by you anymore. You may say "one day I may use it" but that one day may never come and it's sitting on a shelf wasting space and wasting money. Once a sound budget is set up repurchasing a similar item may be an option, a newer version but right now it's collecting dust. There are many options to sell your unwanted items such as a yard sale, eBay or Craigslist. Use the money you gain from these sells to pay an old debt or to pay off a credit card. You'll feel a sense of accomplishment once you no longer worry about sending money to a creditor for an interest payment without impacting the principal amount you placed on the credit account.

RETURN IT BEFORE YOU BUY IT

This is a very important step and will change your outlook on financial management giving you the motivation to continue this plan. When you go to a store and place an item in the cart you find unnecessary, put the item back and take the money you would've paid for that item and put it in a savings account. You would have paid for this item thoughtlessly so putting the money in a savings account will teach you that discipline in your spending habits has great rewards. I call this habit "Feeding the Pig" which I named after I noticed when I spent money thoughtlessly on items I didn't need. I was feeding my want to buy items that enticed me, so instead of feeding this desire I began to "Feed the Pig" instead, my savings account. This solution applies to any spending you find unnecessary. If you limit your smoking or quit your addictions the money you spend on the days you would've bought these products needs to be placed in a savings account. You notice that making this a habit will increase your savings account giving you the motivation and excitement to change your lifestyle and spending habits.

When saving your money, you don't want to forget to get paid for saving. Many banks offer savings accounts that offer interest payments for using the funds you place in select savings accounts. I encourage you to find these banks and start a savings account with them that accumulates interest for your saving efforts. When you have this account set up each year place your tax return in the account. Most tax returns are ranging from a couple hundred dollars to a couple thousand. Even though the interest on these savings account appear low, any extra money they pay for your saving habits is free money. If you see your balance increasing and you want another way for interest to be added for your efforts you can ask for information from a bank such as pamphlets showing the benefits of CDs and other investment options. The only downfall to a CD is the inability to withdrawal the funds if an emergency should arise. There are other ways to gain interest from financial institutions but research and speaking with a financial expert will assure you find the best choice that suites your individual needs.

As you see this chapter focuses on increasing your savings potential. We discussed the debt solutions but creating a plan for savings is crucial. Now you aren't tossing your money out of the window so what to do with it next? You need to learn to save and find every source of income available for your savings account. When I was financially struggling and tried to pull myself out of the hole I was with my kids in the living room playing with their toys and I was creating my first budget, thinking to myself the most effective way to pay off debt and start a good savings plan. I did the math and thought with an intelligent mind this plan I am discussing now when my daughter went upstairs without me knowing. She was young almost four, so I went upstairs looking for her and found her in her room with a ceramic pig, putting pennies in the hole on the top. After seeing this I discovered another savings that is overlooked everyday by most people. I'd never take from my daughter but curious I sat with her and dumped her coins out on the floor of her bedroom. We separated them and counted every coin and it came to $68. This looks like an insignificant amount for savings but this money we thought was useless. A penny here and a nickel there, leaving coins on the counter for it to be put in a drawer later. These coins appear so small in value but my daughter had the great idea, collect the change and put it in the bank. I still give her my change but if you don't have a child interested in collecting your pennies put all of your change in a container. Once the container is full, spend a few hours separating the coins and rolling them in coin paper. It will amaze you how rapidly this "useless" change will be a great addition to your savings account.

GOLDEN TICKET: CREATE YOUR BUDGET

Now we've discussed the debt solutions and what to do with your money once you're ready to save, now I'll show you how to make a budget. This is the most important part of this book because without a budget you are irresponsibly spending your hard earned money. The first thing to do is gather your bills from creditors together. Now I say all your bills from creditors but I am not saying the ones you pay every month but also the ones that have fallen into the delinquent bracket. After you place your creditor accounts in front of you get a piece of paper. List the priorities you need to live or receive a paycheck. Examples of this are categories such as your mortgage or rent, you cannot live without a roof covering your head. So I can give you a list and if they apply to you write them on a sheet of paper; mortgage/rent, groceries, gasoline, auto insurance (if required) to name a few. After that is completed write down the credit accounts such as credit cards or any outstanding loans that cannot be negotiated because they are being paid on and open accounts. List them according to their remaining balances starting with the smallest balance and listed in ascending order. Once you are done with that you can list your contracted accounts from providers such as mobile accounts, cable television or satellite. Once that is listed you can list any other obligations you pay that are not delinquent. List your delinquent accounts so you can save funds to pay these off once you take care of your current credit cards and loans. Last List a saving's category at the end. This is not a last priority but you will not be using this category to its full potential yet.

Now everything's listed to be placed in a budget but now you need to apply it to a format that is manageable and understandable. There are many options to apply these categories from book logs to software. I use software but I have also created my own using Microsoft Excel. If you prefer a hard copy, go to any retail department store and you will most likely find a budget book in the office supplies. So depending on whether you want to invest in software that gives you an up to date record of your current spending habits or you want to create a spending plan on your own, software or a spreadsheet would be my recommendation. The key is to see what works best for you and begin your budget while you are motivated to change your financial future. After you choose the budgeting format you will work with, place the month on the top of the budget. On the Expenses copy in order everything you wrote on the plain sheet of paper. At the bottom of the budget log your income if it's a predictable amount. Do not include overtime. This is not a reliable source of income so you cannot add it to your budget. Place the payments next to the expense that are predictable. These are payments that are the same from month to month such as your mortgage or rent and your cell phone bill. Once those are listed, place an allotment on your groceries for the month and your gasoline use for the month. You should have a rough idea of how much you spend each month on these expenses. Add both the predictable amounts and the groceries and gasoline allotments together. This figure is what you are spending with these payments. Subtract this from your income as soon as you know what your income will be. look at your statements and find your unpredictable bills such as credit cards and place the minimum amount due in the areas on your budget. Subtract this from what was remaining of your monthly income and disperse the remaining funds from your income. Start with your lowest Credit account because this is the first you want to pay off. You'll want to place a quantity in the category of your savings. This amount need not be a large sum because right now we are placing funds in your savings for general vehicle and home maintenance and emergencies. The focus should be to get your debts paid. Once you begin your budget it may be necessary to go back several times to adjust the allotments to each category. If you find that your grocery needs are consistently going over your budgeted allotment adjust it as needed but keep the adjustments suitable towards your savings goal.

    I told you that once your credit cards are paid off to keep them for use and that I would talk about how your credit cards should be used to your full benefit so we will discuss this method. You never know when you will need your credit so keeping your scores to an above average or excellent level is very important to keep your credit in good terms. Your credit cards should never be used over what you can pay. Use your credit cards for your everyday needs like gasoline or groceries. Remember that this isn't extra money that can be added to your budget. You have to pay this back so when you pay for gas using your credit card put that amount in your savings account. When you go to a grocery store and use your credit card, stop by the bank on the way home and put that money in your savings account. This is a free way to raise your credit. When your credit card bill comes in you see that balance matches the amount you put into savings. Retrieve those funds from your savings account and pay off your credit card . There should be a zero balance every month on your credit cards.

To motivate you to finish and keep a correct and efficient budget and use your credit sensibly you need to set goals. Make sure your goals are realistic by starting small. Think of 4-5 goals which are out of your reach to do as of right now. This will motivate you to stick with your plan and focus on your future wants instead of your impulsive desires. Once you can accomplish paying your debts and began the saving process you will be ready to focus on achieving your goals. Never stop making goals because they will be your motivation to continue good financial practices.

PLAN FOR THE BEST, PREPARE FOR THE WORST

Personal finances are a constant work in progress, remember that. Life will put circumstances and road blocks in your way causing you to become frustrated with the budgeting route. Keep focused on your future desires and the joy of knowing you have money in the bank at your disposal. Once you are ready to start your savings you need to categorize your savings account. Each month you should see balances on debts decreasing and falling off the budget once they are paid in full. Put categories into your savings account using your budget, this will give you the opportunity to know what you are saving towards. You can put "Vacation" or "New Car" you do not want to leave out "Emergency" Life will put roadblocks in your way causing frustration because you may face a situation that will cost you a large amount of your savings. Saving for this category in particular will take the burden off of your other savings categories.

Whether other categories are for new vehicles or a vacation you need to know what you want and go after it. It is in your grasp as long as you display the determination to change your way of thinking about your paycheck and where it goes. Long term planning is a great way to learn to save, securing your financial security for retirement. Retirement from SSI and other pension plans has decreased over the years and inflation is a constant. Consider investment options such as a 401k or other pension plans to make sure your savings plans are reaching their full potential.

Research and learn how millionaires stay millionaires and you will learn the key to keeping your money. A responsible millionaire doesn't buy a brand new car that has never left the manufacturers retailers lot. They buy a vehicle that has was drove off the lot because depreciation is money lost. When buying clothes don't worry about the name brand. No one is walking up to you and looking down your shirt or pants to see what brand shirt or pants you are wearing. Think logically with your purchases this the best way to keep money in your pocket. Carefully manage your budget and feel accomplished that you are taking a step towards a better financial life. This is a frustrating procedure but a rewarding one, a breath of fresh air. So breathe deep, get serious, pay your debts off and save your paychecks. Feed the Pig!

www.ingramcontent.com/pod-product-compliance
Lightning Source LLC
Chambersburg PA
CBHW071017180526
45168CB00003B/1459